Coaching Little Kid Soccer

The easy, fun way to teach youth soccer skills to 3-year-old, 4-year-old, 5-year-old and 6-year-old preschoolers & kindergarteners

BRYAN GILMER

This book is offered as a way to help adults think about coaching kids' soccer. It reflects the author's opinions and is for educational purposes only. Readers should use caution and good judgment and make their own decisions, as they are responsible for ensuring their personal safety and the safety of their own team. Coaches should follow league rules and guidelines at all times. Children's names in the text, except for the author's son Quinn, are fictitious to protect the privacy of children coached. Hillandale Sports Association did not authorize this book nor contribute to it, and all views expressed are solely those of the author.

Gilmer, Bryan, 1972–
Coaching Little Kid Soccer: The easy, fun way to teach youth soccer skills to 3-year-old, 4-year-old, 5-year-old and 6-year-old preschoolers and kindergarteners
/ Bryan Gilmer – 1st ed.

Printed in the United States of America

10 9 8 7 6 5 4 3 2 1

First Edition

For Quinn

Contents

1

How I first thought I wasn't qualified to coach little kid soccer – and ended up writing a coaching book

Hi, I'm Bryan Gilmer. Quinn's dad.

The first season he played recreational soccer here in Durham, North Carolina, he was 4. When we registered him with the Hillandale Sports Association, I didn't check the box to volunteer as a coach, even though I was kind of interested in doing it. First, I had no experience coaching. Second, I have never been much of an athlete – my favorite outdoor activity is hiking. In short, I figured I probably wasn't qualified and that there would be some expert jock parent in the group who would teach him and his teammates everything they needed to know. I figured I would just leave it to that person and maybe help out if I was needed.

But that first season – that very first practice – as I watched from the sideline, I thought to myself, "This isn't the right way to work with kids this age at all!" The coach, an incredibly kind and good-hearted guy about my age, was running drills with them where they had to stand in line and wait their turn and then complete a series of tasks – only to return to the back of the line for another two-minute wait. The kids were not only fidgeting and losing interest; they were antagonizing each other and starting conflicts. The coach would alternately ignore that behavior and admonish the kids to stand still and wait their turn.

Quinn is a particularly high-energy kid. And every parent quickly learns that you can create circumstances for your child that make them likely to succeed, or you can impose unreasonable expectations and watch as the child fails spectacularly. Good parenting is a balance between stretching your child to expand his limits and not setting her up to fail. Kelly and I have always known that Quinn needs to get physically tired every day.

So I felt convinced that he and these teammates needed to be running and moving – doing. Instead, Quinn finished that first practice without breaking a sweat. Soccer was kind of a shrug for him, as a result. A time to be squirmy for an hour. I wanted him to love playing like I had for eight or nine years as a kid, even though I'd never been very good (nor started nearly that young). I thought, "If I was coach, I'd have those kids moving every minute of practice. I'd call the drills 'games' and make them playful and choose or design games that involved all the kids at once."

Why *wasn't* there someone better qualified than me coaching Quinn's team? I realize now that it's because parents learn from scratch to become coaches just like kids learn from scratch to play the sport. You can begin now by coaching your own kid's teams from the youngest age that he or she plays, and then you can progress through the sport with them over the years for as long as you enjoy it.

As we played all the other teams in the league that first season, I saw that except for a couple of parents who had older kids in addition to their 4-year-old, really none of the coaches had any experience, either. Many of them, in fact, felt roped into coaching because no one else had volunteered and someone from the league had come begging. (And those few experienced

2

parent coaches among us tended to be coaching the older siblings' teams!) Some of these novices were doing a valiant job, but many of them were struggling to lead their teams, keep the kids engaged, and even to have a good time themselves.

The next season, I ended up volunteering to be an assistant coach – but because the volunteer coach felt so unprepared, she basically asked me to take over.

And I began feeling my way, developing what turned into a comprehensive philosophy and method for guiding preschoolers and kindergarteners into soccer – a method that the kids and parents have liked so much that several families have requested me to be their child's coach again in a new season.

So I'm here to tell you that you have everything you need to coach your son's or daughter's soccer team: You understand where your child and her peers are developmentally. You want them to be healthy and get exercise and learn to work as part of a team and to follow instructions and overcome adversity. You may or may not be athletic (I am essentially a professional sitter-at-a-desk).

It doesn't matter. For a preschool through kindergarten team, you can be a good coach – a great coach – with zero experience or even initial knowledge of soccer.

In this book, I'm giving you everything I've picked up from other coaches and the kids themselves while coaching Quinn and his teammates. I believe it will get you started with confidence.

2

Your coaching mindset

Professional soccer – or even high-school age soccer – is an elegant combination of marathon running and chess. Huge teams, lots of specialized roles or positions on the teams, airborne balls flying fifty yards, goalkeepers diving on the ground, all on a vast expanse of manicured turf. Teams using complicated strategies that require each player to be smart and aware and to anticipate where each of his teammates might be 10 seconds into the future. There are goal kicks, corner kicks, throw ins, and goalie punts. Maybe it's this image of soccer that made you intimidated about coaching little kid soccer.

Understanding the game of little kid soccer

Little kid soccer is far simpler. It's played "short-sided," that is with only three or four of each side's (the British term for a soccer team) players on the field at one time. It is usually co-ed; the coaches are usually on the field, and there shouldn't be goalies. In our league, we don't keep score, either.

I can tell all you about little kid soccer in four sentences, even if you've never seen soccer played before: It's life-size arcade air hockey. There's a ball, a weedy rectangle the size of sixteen parking spaces, and an open net at each end. Our team wants the ball to go into that net and stay out of this one. If one team makes the ball go out of bounds, the other team gets to kick it back in.

Seriously, that's the whole thing. That means that coaching little kid soccer requires zero complicated strategy. It is entirely focused on giving kids basic skills, encouragement, and a very simple set of instructions. And helping them to have a blast mastering it all.

Offense: On offense, your kids need to know how to dribble, or use their feet to control the ball while they walk or run with it to get it close to the other team's goal. And then they need to know how to shoot the ball, that is, to kick it so that it goes into the other team's goal.

What about passing? Uh-uh. You can show them in practice how to pass the ball to a teammate, and you should, but that's preparation for the next level. I have never seen a successful pass between teammates in the course of a little kid soccer game. At least, not an intentional pass! (Okay, I do have my kids start play at the kickoff with a little tap pass to a teammate.) But a pass in the course of play is just beyond their anticipation and coordination abilities at this age. Plus, they are so self-centered that when they get the ball, the only thing they can think of is how to score it themselves.

And listen to me: That is just fine. It is perfect, because it's honestly where they are. Knowing and accepting these kinds of things about the kids on our team helps us be great coaches for them.

So, envision that one kid on your team has the ball and is dribbling toward the other team's goal, just like you taught her. Fantastic. What about her teammates who don't have the ball? Their job is to (and here's the first of several catch phrases I'll teach you to shout) "Run with her!" They run down the field several feet to each side of and slightly behind the ball handler, and if she loses possession, they try to get and complete the team's job of scoring. You will need to teach them at first not to try to take the ball away from her. ("She's on your team! Don't take it away; cooperate!")

Defense: Most of what you might call little kid soccer strategy happens on defense.

The first thing they need to learn is that when a kid on the other team has the ball, we want to get between that kid and our goal. So say we're trying to score and we lose possession of the ball. Your players' job is to run fast to get between the kid with the ball and your goal. ("Get between!")

The other element of strategy that works is keeping the ball from rolling near the mouth of our goal. In practice, I put cones on the field to mark out the width of the goal about 15 feet into the field. I call this lane in the very center of the field at the mouth of our goal, "our rectangle," and I teach kids, "Keep it out of our rectangle!" During a game, they easily remember where that area is without the cones.

If an opposing player is dribbling straight toward our goal, we want to stop him before the ball gets inside our imaginary rectangle. If a player kicks the ball sideways across the mouth of our goal where a teammate might be able to shoot it, we kick it away. If you recover the ball to one side of our goal, don't kick or dribble it into our rectangle! ("Take it up the field!")

Of course, when we're on offense, we *want* the ball in the middle of the field, *in* the other team's rectangle, as the first step toward putting it into their goal.

Guess what? Having just read that, you could easily stand in for me this Saturday and coach my team. That's how simple it is.

Understand this age and each child

Try to put yourself in the mindset of each child at each practice and game. Remember being this age yourself, and think

7

of what your own child this age has taught you so far. For many of them, participating in an organized activity is a complete first. Some are uncertain, and some are terrified. Most have no real idea what to do or how they should behave. You will gently teach them all of this. And they will not so gently show you what you need to learn as a coach – if you are open to learning and perceptive enough to realize.

Get to know each child. At the first practice, as kids arrive, meet them and their parents as they walk up to the field and have a little conversation with each one. Get down to the child's eye level and introduce yourself. I am 6-foot-3, 210 pounds, so the tip is especially important for me. The conversation goes like this:

"Hi, my name is Coach Bryan. I'm going to teach you about playing soccer. What's your name?"

"Jacob."

"Hey, Jacob. How old are you?"

Jacob may solemnly hold up four fingers. He may say, "Four; I have a sister who's 2 and she's a baby and my special stuffed dog is named Donnie. How old are you?" He might flee behind his mom's legs for protection from this big, scary man he does not know. Right away as coach, I'm starting to get a sense of the child's level of shyness or outgoing-ness, developmental level, and so forth. The other thing I want to know right away is if the kid has played soccer before.

A conversation with a strange new grownup whose attention is completely on the child is pretty intense for them. So I keep it to those couple of questions. Then I stretch out my hand to the child and say, "Come on, let's go meet your new friends and play." The kid looks to his mom or dad to make sure this is okay, and when the parent nods, I stand and lead him by the hand into the group, where I tell everyone their name, and they shyly wave at each other.

All through the season, you want to keep tabs on each particular child, what they are struggling with, what they find fulfilling, and what you can help them work on. A kid with prior soccer experience needs to take her dribbling skills to the next level. A boy who falls down a lot needs to learn to balance or at least to hop back up. An aggressive child may need to channel that appropriately into the game instead of into pushing. Jonathan may need to keep the ball closer to his feet while he dribbles to maintain control, while Catherine may need your encouragement to try to move a little faster with it. Also, before the season, I email parents and ask them to tell me if their child has any special needs: physical disabilities, autism, developmental delays, peanut allergies, diabetes, etc.

So, even though I'm about to advise you to do lots of big-group activities with the kids so they all stay moving most of the time, I encourage you to see each child as an individual with different needs and to tailor your expectations and tips and level of assistance even as you're doing that.

What you're really teaching

It's so easy to get fixated on those soccer skills. And I'll tell you how to teach those in just a little bit.

But remember that the more important things you are teaching kids are abstract concepts that are key to their emotional and psychological development as preschoolers and kindergarteners:

- *That exercise is fun and feels great:* You have the chance to show a generation of kids who will spend unprecedented amounts of time indoors in front of gadget screens that it is delightful and healthy to be outdoors moving your body. One little girl on my team last season came up to me at the end of our first practice slightly alarmed and said, "Coach Bryan, what's this on my skin?" At first, I didn't see anything on her skin. "What do you mean, Jessica?" I asked. "This wet stuff," she said, pointing to the sheen on her forearm. "That is called sweat, Jessica, and when your body makes it, you

9

know you have done a good job of running hard and getting exercise," I replied. It had never happened to her before. I pride myself on sending my kids home pleasantly tired.

- *There are times when it's good to compete:* As I was coaching my very first team, I suddenly realized that the kids were not playing very well because they had been taught by their families that you always have to share and take turns. As a result, some were appalled at the idea of taking the ball away from another player who was dribbling because that must be "not nice." By the same token, you have to teach kids not to be mortally wounded when another player steals the ball from them during the game. ("That's okay! It's part of the game!") They quickly come to understand that different situations in life have different expectations and standards of behavior. You have to be explicit in explaining that to this age.

- *You can learn to manage your feelings:* There are two aspects to how we handle any situation, the way we initially, impulsively feel about it, and the ways we choose to respond to that emotion. The other guy took the ball away from you! You're mad about it! You can flop down and have a tantrum, or you can run after him and try to get the ball back. There's a lot of trial and error on these things with younger children; the important thing is to talk through this thought process with them again and again. Validate their feeling: "You were so frustrated when he stole it away! But you must not throw your shoe at him because that could hurt him. What else could you have done instead?"

- *We persevere through adversity:* Especially if you're coaching middle-class kids, many of them have not experienced – or learned to overcome – much hardship.

10

But a little bit of manageable hardship develops the crucial life skill of positive perseverance. I find myself constantly telling my kids things like, "Yes, we have been playing hard, and your body feels tired. But Alvin, I don't think it's true that you can't play any more. Even though your body is tired, it is strong enough to keep going if you really try." Or, "You bumped your finger on the goal, and it did not feel good, but there is no blood and you can wiggle it. You are okay."

Kids are amazed and so satisfied when they find they can overcome a little setback or do a little bit more than they thought they could, or that they don't have to melt into a puddle over every discomfort and minor disappointment. Obviously, you have to use sound judgment. If a kid is having a heat stroke, or is bleeding, or severely upset, don't tell them to power through. It's that same principle of stretching them just a little bit but never pushing them.

• *We need to learn to cooperate as part of a team:* Kids need to learn that sometimes I am the one who scores the goal for my team, and sometimes Rico is. That the coach is their leader, and that they follow Coach's instructions and ask Coach questions when they are not sure.

That even though they don't find it easy to get along with Tina, she is on their team and so they have to work through their conflicts so we can all be successful together. Which probably sounds a lot like the skills you need for your day job.

3

Bryan's first principles

Realizing all of this has led me to a few principles I try to keep in mind at all times while coaching kids in this age range:

- ***Do it with them. Model the behavior you seek.*** You, the coach, need to be out on the field with the kids at practice. You dribble the ball to show them how. If you want the team to run, run with them. If you're in poor shape, at least run with them the first time to show them rather than tell them.

- ***Keep it fun!*** Don't practice dribbling when you can play tap, tap, tap the dinosaur egg. Don't all dribble in a line behind each other when you can dribble in the shape of a snake or pretend to be a train. Smile and laugh with them. Use cartoon voices. Bump fists or high-five with them when the team does something great – my trademark is a gentle fist bump with the child with me saying "Boop!" in a high-pitched voice as I do it. We use this to celebrate goals (bump with everyone

13

on the team) or personal breakthroughs. Cheer extravagantly when they achieve milestones. This is playtime. Sometimes, your instructions need to be serious, but often they can be playful and funny.

- *Expect the kids to perform to their abilities.* As I've already explained, you want them to perform as best they can and work on getting better, not to let them get away with underperforming. You pay a child a compliment when you ask her for her best. One debate I got into with our league commissioner was whether to enforce out of bounds. His thought was, just let them play; why stop the action?

  But at some point, they're so far from the field that you have to. Then they wonder, why is 10 feet out of bounds okay but 20 isn't? I argued that there's a line around the field, and the kids can easily see and understand it, and it is not expecting too much to ask them to observe it. If the ball strays a foot out of bounds and comes back in, sure, let them play. But if it shoots out of bounds, let's stop and let them kick it in. If they don't like stopping, they'll be careful not to let it go out of bounds next time. That level of structure is very helpful to this age of child.

- *Assume nothing.* You cannot assume that any child on your team knows a single thing about soccer or team sports. Time after time, I see coaches getting frustrated because they are assuming that the kids know simple things that they simply don't know – because no one ever told the child. Coaches of this age have to make everything pretty explicit. For example, "This big rectangle painted on the ground shows the edges of the field. We have to keep the ball inside here. If it rolls outside the lines, everyone has to stop while we go get it." Or, "Even though basketball has something called drib-

14

bling, and that's also a way to move with the ball, in soccer, we dribble with our feet, not our hands."

- ***Repeat, repeat, repeat.*** If you have ever owned a DVD your child enjoyed, you know that kids not only don't mind repetition at this age but seem to thrive on it. Guess what? It's also true at soccer practice. If your first practice is fun for them, they will happily repeat it verbatim every other practice of the season. I think I started out thinking I would need fresh drills every week. It just isn't true. Repetition leads to mastery. I am going to show you some variations on the practice games I'll teach later on that can help them take their skills to the next level – and make practice a little more interesting for you at the same time.

- ***No false praise.*** This is a real hobbyhorse of mine. I'll spend a whole practice teaching the kids which goal we want the ball to go into, and which one we're trying to keep it out of. Game day rolls around, and Jonathan gets the ball. He dribbles toward our own goal, the one we're supposed to be defending, and kicks the ball into our own net. His mom leads the crowd clapping and cheering: "Good job, Jonathan! Way to go! You made a goal!" She may not realize he messed up. More likely, she's embarrassed that he messed up. Or she may believe that hearing that he messed up will make Jonathan a damaged, resentful child with deep psychological problems.

But actually, it's the other way around. We all make mistakes and need to learn from them. That's what little kid soccer should be all about. I go up to Jonathan, hopefully within the hearing of his mom, and tell him, "Hey buddy, you made a mistake just now by kicking the ball into the wrong goal. We want the ball to go into that goal down there instead. Do you understand? Okay,

15

good. Next time, kick the ball into that net, big boy." Jonathan nods, not scarred for life – and understanding more about how to play soccer. I believe that kids see through false praise and take it as an indication that grownups don't think they're capable enough to do it the right way. I have even gone over to the sidelines and told the mom, "Actually, that wasn't a good job that time. I am not sure you realize, but he kicked the ball into the wrong goal by mistake. Help me encourage him to try for that goal down there. It's okay, we're still learning." And with any luck, the next time Jonathan tries it, the mom is instead shouting, "Other way, Jon!"

4

Team management

Each kid on your team needs:

- **Shin guards:** Each child needs to wear a pair, both in practice and during games. Most leagues require them. Kids are out there kicking at the ball, and they will end up kicking shins when they mean to kick the ball. The Velcro strap kind need to be worn underneath long soccer socks to stay in place.

- **A size-3 soccer ball:** Kids love knowing which ball is theirs, and they can dribble it to the practice field and back to the car, and with any luck will practice with it at home, too. Bigger sizes of ball are too hard for kids this age to manage.

- **Sneakers:** I think cleats are a terrible idea at this age. The kids don't move fast enough to need the extra traction. Plus, they step on each other's feet all the time and kick each other by accident. Cleats will get other kids in

17

the game hurt. (I came home with cuts on my legs after one practice with a kid wearing cleats) Even if your league allows cleats, like ours does, tell your kids to wear soft sneakers. Sandals, dress shoes and Crocs-style shoes all make for poor protection, poor ball control, or poor traction. Don't let kids wear them.

- *Comfortable clothing:* An outfit like sweatpants or shorts and a T-shirt is perfect. Ask parents to put long hair up in a ponytail or braids and leave the princess dresses, Iron Man costumes, chainmail shirts and other bulky clothing at home.

- *Water:* Ask parents to bring a bottle of water for their child, preferably a re-usable one, to be environmentally friendly. Kids don't need sugary athletic beverages (see snack advice later on). And make the rule of no snacks during practice or games (kids stash bites of food in their mouths without Mom or Dad knowing, and when they start to play again, they can choke on it).

What you need, Coach

Your league may supply some or all of this:

- *All of the above,* plus

- *A whistle* (about a dollar at any discount store)

- *Two or three extra size-3 soccer balls* for certain practice games and to share with kids who forget to bring a ball.

- *Practice pinnies,* little colored tank-top overshirts that are a couple bucks apiece you can let the kids wear in practice to group them into teams.

- *Little plastic orange cones,* not the beefy ones they put near potholes, but the flatter ones about the size of a saucer or compact disc that you can use to mark out areas on the field in practice. In fact, you could use unwanted CDs or beanbags.

- *A method of timekeeping.* Your cellphone probably has a timer and stopwatch function on it and will be fine.

- *A mesh bag* to keep it all in.

Involve the other parents

The other parents on your team are sitting there on the sidelines with very little to do. Some of them will have smaller children to manage and be pretty busy. (Though you can still recruit one of those parents to sign each family up for a game day to provide the snack).

Most other parents are very happy to help and to come out onto the field and play with you and the kids during practice. It's a blast to have a physician in his scrubs and a mom in her business suit running around with the kids. Decide exactly what you would like for them to do, and then just ask. If another parent starts trying to take over, just have a friendly conversation telling them you've got a progression in mind for the practice.

When you find a parent you work well with, ceremoniously designate her as your official assistant coach (if your league hasn't already assigned you one). This way, if you need to go out of town on game day or practice night, you have someone ready to fill in.

Snacks and drinks

It's a big tradition in many leagues and maybe across America for parents to take turns bringing an after-game snack. But too many times since I've been coaching, this turns out to be little more than a giant dose of high-fructose corn syrup. People buy those kid drinks in the silver pouches with the tiny straw because they're relatively cheap and portable. On one recent game day, a mom brought little packages with chocolate cookies in one end and a sugar paste like sandwich cookie filling in a tub-like compartment at the other end.

I think that's terrible. We're supposed to be teaching kids healthy habits, like getting frequent exercise. What a child who has exercised needs is plenty of water, and not sugar water (and did you know that's what 100-percent fruit juice is, too? Read the nutrition facts – any vitamins you see above 5 percent of Recommended Daily Allowance were added at the factory).

So water is what I want my players to drink. For next season, I've decided to buy a cylindrical drinking water cooler and bring it full to each game and practice to make it easy. (I will also ask each family to bring a reusable cup for their child to drink from so we don't create a mountain of disposable cups.) Or you could just tell each family to bring water for their child, preferably in a reusable bottle or travel cup.

And so I'm instituting a sugary drink and sugary snack ban. It makes no sense to get kids into the habit of reaching for sweets when they exercise. Childhood obesity is (pardon the pun) a huge problem. Let's not teach them to immediately replace all the calories they just burned.

In case you agree, here is a list of healthier but still portable after-game snacks I recommend you ask parents to choose from:

- An actual whole piece of fruit, such as a tangerine, banana, a washed apple or little cup of strawberries or blueberries or grapes, or a mixture. Here you get the skin, the fiber and micronutrients with a much more reasonable-sized portion of juice – and no added sweeteners.

• Baby carrots or celery sticks in a little bathroom-sized paper cup with some hummus or a little ranch dressing at the bottom.

• Whole-grain crackers such as Triscuits with a slice of cheese that has been quartered (not super-processed "singles" cheese but a real slice of cheddar or American.)

• Popcorn.

• Some prepackaged snacks are okay, such as goldfish crackers, Chex Mix, and maybe even a granola bar that's not coated in frosting or chocolate.

Team communication

My league is high-speed enough to provide coaches with a tool to email every parent on the team. (If your league doesn't, get your snack-day organizing parent to collect a list of email addresses for you on the sideline.) I use emails at the beginning of the season to welcome everyone, talk about some of the life lessons we'll be learning, and lay out my draconian snack policy.

During the season, I use group emails to talk about any struggles or accomplishments I see us experiencing and to emphasize the progress the kids are making. In every email, I ask parents to email or call me if they have any questions or concerns about their child, and nearly every time I make this offer, a parent responds (and it's clear they might never have asked if I hadn't extended the offer). Very often, parents apologize for their kids who are having normal issues, and what I end up reassuring them is that it's fine and it happens all the time. If something is a touchy issue, parents are less likely to talk to you at practice or at the game – plus, when you run practice like I advise, you really are too busy the whole time.

Season-end team party

One of my favorite parts of each season is the team party. I usually schedule this for the same evening as our usual practice day right after the season ends. People have the slot blocked out on their calendars and can easily make it. If you don't want to host this at your own house, start asking around to find a family on your team that will. You can make it a potluck or get someone to cook dinner.

In our league, every child gets a trophy. I don't make up a special award for every child like "best dribbler" or "funniest" (see false praise). Instead, I explain that these trophies are a reward for being part of our team and trying hard – and something the kids can keep at home to remember all the fun that we had together. I call each child's name and make a big deal of presenting his or her trophy in front of everyone.

I mention this now only because you should start planning the team party as the season opens.

5

Running practice

When I say running practice, I mean that in both senses of the word: You being in charge, and the kids actually running. I mentioned before that I'm a believer in repetition, and so here's the season-long shape of my typical 50-minute to 1-hour practice (sometimes a little shorter if the kids seem tired, cranky or just over it before the hour is up, and also because in the fall, it gets dark in our part of North Carolina before our hour-long practice window is really finished).

Here are the distinct phases of a Coach Bryan practice.

Prepare your coaching mantras

Get these mantras ready. These are things you will call out dozens and dozens of times during every practice and game:

- *Freeze!*

- *No hands – feet!* Beginners have a compulsion to

reach down and use their hands on the ball when it's not doing what they want. So keep reminding them of this. Even between drills, require them to move their balls around with their feet. Even transition time can be practice time. We never use our hands with our soccer balls at practice.

- *Hop up!* Kids will fall down a lot. When one does, immediately urge her, "Hop up!" It is dangerous in a game for a child to stay on the ground. They can get stepped on, and other kids can fall on top of them. Some kids intentionally dive and roll around on the ground, and you are conditioning them not to do this. When you do get kids trained to hop up instantly – and then one doesn't – you blow the whistle and make everyone freeze and run over to him, because then you know it's probably a real injury.

- *That's okay; try it again!* Offer a specific suggestion on how they might do it, if you're nearby.

- *You did it!*

- *Yeah! Great!*

- *That's right Jolanda, just like that!*

- *Uh, uh, Frankie. We don't do that. No more.*

- *Play friendly!*

Arrival

I try to get to practice five or ten minutes before the official start time. As kids arrive, I say hi to them, give them a

24

"Boop!" fist bump, and invite them to mess around on the field however they want: dribbling, talking to their team friends, shooting on the goal, running around like a crazy person, picking dandelions, whatever.

Stretching

Maybe a minute or two after starting time, I blow the whistle and call all the kids together. Our practices are held on a game field with two goals. We stash all the balls in one of the goals and meet for stretches on the center circle. Any parents and siblings who want to are welcome to join us for stretching. I greet the kids as a group and then lead them through a series of stretching exercises.

Kids this age are so unbelievably flexible that I am sure that stretching is not really necessary. But you know what? All the grownups, including me, who will be playing with them are not. *We* need to stretch so we don't tear a ligament after a long day at the desk. And one day, so will these kids. We're teaching them now that before you play a sport, you take some time to get your body ready, and that good habit will stick with them. This is a concept my buddy Neill Goslin, a much more experienced coach, really sold me on.

Here are the stretches I typically do:

- *"Tall trees":* We all stand on the center circle, feet shoulder width apart, and stretch our arms way high up to the sky. High as you can! Now the wind is blowing – blowing our branches way over to the right! Bend your body to the right! (The kids across the circle will probably mirror you, and that's fine – you should feel your leg muscles and the side muscles of your torso all stretching). Now the wind is changing! It's blowing our branches way over to the left. The wind blows a few more times each direction, and the kids giggle and smile.

25

Then we bend way down and touch our roots, keeping our tree trunk legs straight. They can touch the ground between their feet, then back up, and gently back down to each foot.

Never have kids bounce when stretching; they should always slowly stretch the muscle and then hold it.

- *"Make a letter V with your legs."* If the ground is dry, we sit on the circle, have the kids stretch their legs straight out in front of them like a letter V and press the backs of their knees to the ground. Then they stretch forward to grab the toe of their sneakers and hold on for several seconds. One big problem kids seem to have with this is keeping their legs flat.

  The other is, "Hey, that kind of hurts, coach." So you need to explain that feeling the muscle stretching is good because it means it's working. Remember, you're doing the stretch, too, and you can empathize. "Oh, that feels sore when I do that, right on the back of my leg. But I know that's the way it should feel when I'm getting this muscle ready for exercise. Who else feels that?"

  Look around the circle and compliment each child doing the stretch correctly and offer tips for any who aren't: "Caden, can you get those knees flat so your legs are really straight, like mine are?" Then, have them slowly grab their right foot only, then left foot only.

- *Balance on one foot:* This is about coordination and balance as much as stretching. Have the kids stand on one foot and then bend the other leg up so that their heel touches their bottom – then cradle the laces of their sneaker with their hand. Now, switch legs. This stretches the quads in the front of the leg.

26

- *Hula hoop:* Put your hands on your hips – make a big circle with your hips like you're doing the hula hoop. Now go the opposite direction. Laugh hysterically.

After this point in practice, little brothers and sisters need to be off the field so they don't get hurt and don't reduce the level of play for the kids whose team this is.

Running

A lot of teams that practice near us never just do group running. I suspect this is because the coaches don't want to do it. Guess what? On all my teams, ever, the kids have loved just plain running. Well, it's not really plain – I do it in a fun way.

The kids all like up along one endline, all on the same side of the goal, like racers on the starting line. Only this isn't a race! It's a secret team-building exercise, and best of all, it mimics the flow of the game, where you run up and down the field.

I say, "Everybody jump up and down on this line," and I start pogo-ing up and down on the white endline like I'm trying to bury it. They have a blast doing this, too, and I say, "Ready, set – go!" and we all sprint to the opposite endline. I get there first and jump up and down on that line and tell them to do the same. And here's the key – the fastest kids "wait" there, jumping up and down on that line until ALL the kids have made it down the field. Then I pick a child and say, "Angela, say, 'Ready, set – go!' " And with delight, she'll yell it, and we'll all run back to the other endline, as I shout, "Goooo!" Give a few other kids a turn to be the leader and make at least three trips up and down the field. You can mix it up by sometimes having everyone stop at the midline and then either continue to the opposite endline after everyone gets there or reverse back to the endline where you just were. This teaches them to listen for and to quickly follow your coaching instructions.

Stop when you are winded. The kids will almost certainly want to keep going.

Games for practice

Again, these are not drills. If you design drills, you're working to create drudgery. If you think up games, you're going to come up with activities that do improve the players' skills, but focus on them moving around and having a ball.

Tweet/Go: Here's our first game. We've just been running like crazy. So the first game is going to be a slower-paced one. It lets them rest, and because they have just burned off some energy, they will have a lot more patience for this pace. A really common practice game for this age is called "Red Light/Green Light." When the coach shouts "red light!" everyone freezes where they are, and when she shouts, "Green Light," they can move again.

I've changed it to Tweet/Go. I went to a coaching clinic where the instructor suggested that your first order of business is getting them to freeze when they hear a whistle. I loved the idea because, again, this mimics the flow of the game. So I created "Tweet/Go."

For the first practice, we do this without our soccer balls. The kids simply meander around until they hear your whistle, and then at your tweet, they "Freeze like a statue!" Praise each kid who freezes right away. When you spot one still moving, just grin and point right at them, and they'll freeze, too. The funnier the position they freeze in, the better. You are freezing to model it for them when you blow the whistle. Keep going for several minutes.

By the second or third practice, we play this game dribbling our balls around. When you hear the whistle, you have to stop your ball and put one foot on top of it to keep it still. This is a little harder, and it subtly teaches them that the closer their ball stays to their feet, the more control they have over it, and the faster they can stop it.

Now you tell them, "Any time we're at practice or in a game and you hear my whistle, you freeze and put your foot on top of the ball, just like this." And you know what, it works like crazy. If practice is getting out of hand, at any point, just blow that whistle and point to each kid until she freezes.

Water break! After this game, I shout, "Water break!" and tell the kids to go to their parents and get a sip of water. This should take about 45 seconds, and if you have some sideline stragglers, just call out, "Okay, everybody come back."

Train or snake: Again, for the first practice, I would do this without the ball, just to get the hang of it and very soon I would have them dribble.

For Train, you have them follow you as you walk or dribble along the lines painted on the field as if they were train tracks. You and the kids can make choo-choo noises. Take a hard right-angle turn at the corners. Walk the midline and lead them all the way around the center circle and back the way they came. It's a fun way to learn to follow your directions, and then finally, to control their soccer ball.

Snake is just like train, only you lead them along a random, curvy path across the field, behind the goals, through the parents' sideline chairs, around the bush next to the field, and back to the middle.

A word about dribbling: Some kids will do it by instinct, and others will have a lot of trouble at first. The most helpful advice I have found to offer them is that they need to "tap, tap, tap" the ball with the front inside surface of their feet, just behind the toes. Kids having trouble are usually trying to kick the ball too hard or are trying to use the points of their toes, which offers them no control. The other good tip is, "Tap, follow, tap, follow, tap, follow," to teach them that you nudge the ball forward, move yourself forward, and then tap it again. Both these games make them practice and master dribbling and ball control.

Go Get It: "Everyone bring your ball to me! Make a bunch of grapes right here by my feet!"

You're standing near one end of your practice field. Use

your foot to get one ball from the grapes bunch and kick it far away in a random direction. Tell a child, "Dana, go get it! Dribble it back to me!" She takes off. Immediately kick another ball. "Javier, go get it!" Dana's almost to her ball. Javier has taken off running. You're kicking the next ball and then the next. If you kick the balls far enough and move fast enough, you'll have all the kids moving at every minute of this game. And have you noticed that here is a game where you have all the kids running their hearts out, while you get to stay in one place and rest a little?

Go Get It is another great game where you can add variation and complexity as the season and the kids' skills progress. One of my kids' favorite enhancements is for me to pick up their ball and punt it high into the air instead of just kicking it on the ground. They are learning to control a moving ball, get it into a dribble, and then get it back to the place they want it to go.

Later, instead of bringing the ball back to the grape bunch, you can have each player dribble their ball back past you and shoot it into the goal behind you. (It helps to have an assistant to get the balls out of the net and back to you. If a kid shoots and misses the goal, they run and retrieve their own ball and dribble it back to you). You can also appoint one player as a defender to challenge all the other players as they try to score their goal. Kids usually all want a turn being the defender.

Water break!

Kick the Coach: They've been running like crazy again, so we slow it back down. Tell all the kids to get their balls and start dribbling. Once they're going, you tell them, "Try to kick it right into my feet! Kick the coach!" Devious laughter commences. The first time you play this, you stand still with your feet together, and the kids dribble up to you and kick the ball trying to hit your feet. Many will miss from point blank. If they miss, you can yell, "Close!" or "Ha, you missed me!" and they go retrieve their ball, dribble back and try again. If one hits you, make loud, cartoonish noise, "Ahhh! You got me. Owie, ow, ow, ow! Oh, no, Madison kicked the coach!" (If the ball stops near you, kick it away about 15 feet and they can run get it.)

They won't be able to get enough of this. As they get better, you start moving around very slowly. Later in the season, you can move more quickly. They are learning to couple dribbling in control with stopping the ball and kicking it to a fairly small place that they want it to go. This is secretly practice for shooting into the goal and is preliminary work on passing, where you want the ball to go to your teammate's foot.

Late in the season, you can name one player as your defender. That player tries to stop the other players from kicking you with their ball. The player has a to make a decision about who's the most immediate threat and then quickly figure out how to shut that player down (stand in position and wait for the shot, or go out to the other player and steal the ball with their feet).

Our rectangle: As described in my introduction to little kid soccer earlier, mark out a rectangle the width of the goal about 15 feet into the field. I like to ask all the parents who are interested in participating to stand outside the rectangle and keep the balls rolling into it. The kids all stand in the rectangle and kick the balls back out. You need a lot of grownups, because balls are flying every direction and need to be retrieved.

Then, we switch. It's the parents' rectangle, and it's the kids who try to get the ball to roll into it and the parents who must furiously try to clear them out. Another huge hit. They are learning offensive and defensive strategy, ball control, and how to kick the ball.

A word about kicking: Kids seem to have the instinct to kick the ball with the toe of their shoe. This is painful, and because the toe is curved, offers very little control over where the ball goes. Show the kids how to do a passing-style kick with the instep of their dominant foot. The instep forms a perfect, hockey-stick-shaped cradle that offers great control over where the ball goes. They swing their whole leg like a golf club and push the ball in the direction they want it to go.

For long kicks, teach them to use the laces of their shoe, not the toe. It's worth a little lesson at an early practice and a couple of minutes where they just kick the ball.

Get it from the parents: Now get as many parents onto the field as you can and form a triangle, square, or circle, with the kids in the middle. Have the parents dribble around and kick the ball to each other. Tell all the kids to try to get the ball. (It's kind of like keep-away, but with a whole crowd of kids being "it" all at one time). They will figure out very quickly that they need to get close to the grownup with the ball to try to steal it and cut off her passing angle. Or to position themselves in the passing lanes between grownups. The kids will run around giggling, and when they finally do get hold of a ball, they will be triumphant.

Later in the season, you can have two balls going at once. Water break!

Scrimmage: You probably know that a scrimmage is just a practice soccer game. Give half the kids a practice pinnie. On my teams, there are usually a couple of kids who hate to wear them and about six who are all "Me! Me! Me!" about wearing them. Make sure that at different practices, all the kids who want one get to wear one.

Now divide into two teams. If only seven kids showed up, put your best player on a team with two other players against four medium players. The uneven team size doesn't matter much because the game is still so much about one player trying to score solo.

The first time you do it, have circle time on the center circle and explain how to play the game to them. If you realize later you forgot to say something, you can blow the whistle, get everyone to freeze, and then explain it.

I like to end most practices with a scrimmage, and I try to spend at least 20 minutes on it. It gives the kids the chance to put together all the new skills they have learned in the other games in the context of the standard game of soccer. If you only have one practice before your first game, you may feel doubt-ful about letting them scrimmage that first practice when every-thing seems so rough. But would you rather them try it for the first time on game day? They will arrive much more confident on game day if they've already tried it.

Begin by getting each little team together. Get down on their level. Tell them all, "We want the ball to go into that goal." Make them all point to it. "We want to STOP the ball from go-ing into THAT goal." Point to the defensive goal. Then do the same with the other team. Then, let one team kick off from the center circle with a little pass to a teammate.

Then, pretty much let them play, with a minimum of coaching. Allow them space to experiment and find out what works and what doesn't. If I let him dribble past me, he can eas-ily score. If I let the ball get too far out in front of me on the dribble, someone can steal it.

Later in the season, I'll use a scrimmage to emphasize de-fense. I will show players how they stay between the attacking player and their own goal. How to "Get close to him!" or close in on the player with the ball to provide pressure and "Make him see a small goal," that is, one where most of the possible angles are blocked by the defender.

And with experienced players or late in the season, I will even assign one player on each team to stay back on the defen-sive end all the time and play the position of defender. This is a very popular job. Kids with a knack for this may go on to be-come defenders or goalies at higher levels of soccer.

On game days, I have had other coaches object once or twice that there are supposed to be "no goalies" in this league. I agree, but I point out my defender is only using her feet and that it is good to introduce the idea of different positions and roles. It does cut down on breakaway goals by the other team to have someone hanging back like that, which was probably the source of the objections.

Circle time

I end every practice with circle time – and this time, I hold it over by the sideline where all the parents have been watching. I want them to overhear what I'm emphasizing with the kids. I remind the kids what they learned, that they got great exercise. I tell them the time and field of our upcoming game and tell them how much fun it will be. I take any questions the kids have, and I tell them a couple of things they can think about or practice at home on their own or with their siblings or parent.

Then we do "Hands in the middle," and when I say "One, two, three," we all yell our team name.

6

Game-day coaching

On game day, get to the field 10 minutes early. As kids arrive, greet them and direct them to mess around on our end of the field.

Make a point to meet and speak to the other team's coaches, who will be on the field running the game with you.

Talk about:

- Who will keep time.

- How you will enforce the rules (here I mention to them that I do like to enforce out-of-bounds pretty strictly for the reasons I already mentioned).

- Talk about any problems such as not enough players. If one team is short while the other has plenty, loan some players out.

- Try to build a rapport so that you can work together

during the game to keep play friendly and fun and so you seem like a nice enough person that they won't mind if you offer a word or two of advice to their player.

As start time approaches, do stretching with the team as in practice. Quietly tell the four players you will start that they will go first. Tell the others that they will have a break first and come in when you call their names. It is good to have your assistant coach or a parent keep track of which kids have not played very much and to point that out to you when you're looking for a sub during the game.

In Hillandale Sports Association, we have some guidelines about when substitutions happen, but in real life, mini-crises, post-goal celebrations with dad and other eventualities mean that we're substituting willy-nilly for most of the game in a heroic effort to keep four players on the field at all times.

Troubleshooting

Certain problems tend to come up in games, but some of these may happen in practice, too. Here's a guide for handling them:

A kid refuses to play. This happens a lot at this age level. Kids go on instantaneous strike for a lot of reasons: Shyness, grumpiness, hungriness, tiredness, irritation, or strong emotions about what just happened on the field that a child needs a couple of minutes to process.

So listen: If a kid does not want to play at a particular moment, don't force him. Continually invite her to participate ("Jacqueline, it's your turn now, come on out here." "How are you doing, Nathan? Ready to try again?") But if they decline, let them sit with their parents on the sideline. You will usually have to signal the parents not to push too much and persuade them that it's fine for the child to wait to be comfortable returning to play. I tell the parent or parents, "Let Jacob watch for a couple of minutes, and have him come join us when he's ready."

For some reason, the parents of shy kids tend to be the pushiest of all. The shyest kids I have ever coached have all eventually become enthusiastic players; they just needed some respect for who they are and time to get comfortable, and then they were just fine.

Something else I've learned is not to call across the field to shy kids, something I got wrong a lot at first as a natural extrovert myself. I'm hollering over to kids, and they're going into hiding behind their dad's camp chair. Finally I got the picture one day. Calling out to a shy child in front of everyone makes him retract his head and limbs into his turtle shell. With a very shy kid, I walk up to the child, get down on her level, and speak to her very quietly. Respecting shy kids' temperament in this way almost always helps to win their trust and cooperation.

A parent is obnoxious. Game day can bring out the competitive streak in parents. They may be overly hard on their own kids, in which case I quietly tell the parent, "She's doing just fine. Let's keep it nice and positive." Or they may be overly defensive when another player challenges their child on the field, which might cause me to promise, "I'm keeping an eye on that. It looks like everybody's playing fair right now, but if it gets rough, I'll say something."

Another possible issue is a parent directing their own child or even other kids on your team about what to do from the sidelines – when their instructions contradict what you've been trying to teach. I like to go over with a smile and say, "I see you're really excited, but I have actually been trying to get them to do this." Usually, the parent sheepishly tells you he didn't realize he was screaming out instructions, and they'll be quiet after that.

A child is rough. Game day tends to bring out the aggression in the kids, too. Try to spot overly rough behavior early, and say something about it right away. "Don't put your hands on the other player!" "Use your feet to get the ball!" "No pushing!" "Don't trip people!"

If your player is having trouble controlling himself after repeated warnings – or commits a serious infraction such as shoving another kid to the ground hard, blow your whistle, go over, and sternly order the child to take a break with their parent on the sidelines. This emphasizes that such behavior isn't acceptable and gives the kid time to work through strong feelings with their parent and then to simmer down. Expect the opposing coach to govern her players the same way, and if she doesn't, ask her to take the action you think is appropriate, or speak to the opposing player yourself.

If two kids seem to be personally antagonizing each other (and it tends to happen between especially competitive players), I like to get them together in a little 4-footer huddle and point out their behaviors and why they are not acceptable: "Jamie, when you pushed him, he fell down and that made him angry. Then when he came over and yanked your jersey, you didn't like that. Let's treat each other with respect and let's focus on getting the soccer ball and using our feet to do it. Do you understand?" And get a head nod or a yes from each player. You can also direct each player to apologize to the other if it seems appopriate.

Kids will quickly get the picture that there will be no nonsense allowed.

Coaching your own son or daughter. This is a weird experience for your child, because now you're in a somewhat different role than they're used to you occupying in their life. You own child may become jealous at all the attention you're giving to the other players. It is great if you have a spouse or partner who can come to practices and games also. That way, your child has Coach Daddy or Coach Mommy on the field, and a 100-percent parent waiting on the sideline. This is good for you, too, because you can keep your attention on all the kids in your care while knowing your own is being well tended to.

The other thing is that I believe most coaches tend to be

far less patient and understanding with their own children than with the others on the team. And I know that in my case, this has led me to be unfairly harsh with Quinn – and I think he has sensed that unfairness and felt hurt over it. One thing is that I know when he's really stumped and when he just isn't trying. In the same situation with another kid, I wouldn't be sure, and so I would offer the benefit of the doubt.

The other dynamic is that is embarrassing for you as the coach when your own child doesn't follow your instructions or doesn't handle adversity well. Here you are trying to model positive, appropriate behavior for your team and all these other parents, and your own kid is the one who is doing the opposite.

But you have to remember that in this sense, your kid really is just another kid on the team, and you're teaching them, too, and that the other parents know from experience how this sort of thing goes. Sometimes, you get pushback and especially poor behavior from your own child because of the jealousy dynamic above (other kids have come up to hug my legs at practice, and Quinn has reproached them: "That is MY daddy.") Even though you are busy coaching, you have to be sure to go over and spend a few parental moments with your child from time to time so they know that they are special to you.

A child gets hurt or injured. As I indicated above, you have to get good at triaging bumps versus genuine injuries. Kids are usually excellent judges of which it is, and you let them make the call what level of treatment they need. Say a kid bangs knees with another player, or falls down, or bumps heads, or collides with a teammate.

I go through this progression:

- "Hop up, Jaden! You okay?" If yes, life goes on

- If Jaden doesn't hop up, I whistle a stop to play and go check on him.

- If Jaden's crying and gets up but doesn't rejoin the game, or points to the part of his body that is smarting, I go over and ask: "Is there any blood? Can you move it? Have you tried shaking it a little bit?" Play may be continuing elsewhere on the field.

- If he seems to be feeling better now, I ask, "What do you think, Jaden, can you keep playing?" If Jaden says yes, I pat him on the shoulder and direct him back into the action. It is excellent training in resilience for kids to learn to overcome minor bumps and discomforts without the aid of their parent.

- It is NOT excellent training in resilience to push a child to do so beyond his level of ability. So if he says he is not ready to play, I send him to the sideline and say, "Go let your dad see about it," and call for a sub.

Obviously, follow your league procedures, the parent's wishes and your own common sense if a serious injury occurs. Happily, nothing even close has ever happened in my tenure as coach.

Parent tunnel

We have a great tradition in Hillandale Sports Association for the end of the game. We have the kids line up on the midline and shake hands with each other. Then one of us coaches will holler, "Parent tunnel!" and gesture to the sidelines for all the parents to come onto the field and join us.

The parents form two rows and face each other, each grownup pressing our hands against the person's in the row opposite us. This creates a little tunnel for the kids to run through from end to end, which they do with delight while we whoop our appreciation for their effort.

Maybe you have something similar in your league already. If not, why not try to get it started?

7

You'll figure it out

Coaching Quinn's soccer teams is some of the best fun I have these days. In fact, getting silly with him and his teammates and having fun doing it has caused me to get silly with him more often at home, one on one.

Now I've told you how I approach the game. If anything I've said doesn't make sense, ring true, or work for you or your team, you should discard it or modify it. You will certainly think of ideas that are better than mine and invent your own games (and when you do, I hope you e-mail to tell me about them).

What I hope you do take away from my approach is a way of tailoring your coaching style to meet the needs of your team. Notice that I said needs rather than wants. When you have your players' best interests at hearts, and they can sense that, it builds loyalty and trust. So does you taking the time to get to know each of them and being willing to have fun and be playful with them. Then, when you ask them to stretch themselves just a little bit through a tough situation in a game or practice, they are willing to try to do it even though it's scary and uncertain. And they come out feeling stronger, more capable, and just a little more prepared for the future.

43

I hope I've been able to offer something like expertise that you can use in coaching your team. But when it comes down to it, I'm no expert. I'm just another parent, like you, who wants the best for my child and sees a good experience in youth sports as a great way to help him grow up the right way.

I know that you'll make sure that's the case for your team, too. It's important work. Have a great time, and try not to tear your ACL!

ABOUT THE AUTHOR

Bryan Gilmer has made his living as a writer for more than 18 years, working first as a newspaper reporter in Greenville, South Carolina, before moving on to Florida's largest newspaper, the St. Petersburg Times. Now he works as a consultant writing for institutional and corporate clients, in addition to writing crime thriller novels for an adult audience. They include **Kill the Story**, a mystery, and **Felonious Jazz**, a thriller.

Bryan lives with his wife, Kelly, and their son, Quinn, in Durham, North Carolina.

E-mail him at bryan@bryangilmer.com; visit his website at BryanGilmer.com; subscribe to his feed on Facebook; or follow him on Twitter: @BryanGilmer.

50322277R00032

Made in the USA
San Bernardino, CA
19 June 2017